MURMURATION

THE HUGH MacLENNAN POETRY SERIES

Editors: Allan Hepburn and Carolyn Smart

Recent titles in the series

rushes from the river disappointment stephanie roberts
A House in Memory David Helwig
Side Effects May Include Strangers Dominik Parisien
Check Sarah Tolmie
The Milk of Amnesia Danielle Janess
Field Guide to the Lost Flower of Crete Eleonore
    Schönmaier
Unbound Gabrielle McIntire
Ripping down half the trees Evan J
whereabouts Edward Carson
The Tantramar Re-Vision Kevin Irie
Earth Words: Conversing with Three Sages John Reibetanz
Vlarf Jason Camlot
Unbecoming Neil Surkan
Bitter in the Belly John Emil Vincent
unfinishing Brian Henderson
Nuclear Family Jean Van Loon
Full Moon of Afraid and Craving Melanie Power
Rags of Night in Our Mouths Margo Wheaton
watching for life David Zieroth
Orchid Heart Elegies Zoë Landale
The House You Were Born In Tanya Standish McIntyre
The Decline and Fall of the Chatty Empire
    John Emil Vincent
New Songs for Orpheus John Reibetanz
the swailing Patrick James Errington
movingparts Edward Carson
Murmuration: Marianne's Book John Baglow

Murmuration
Marianne's Book

JOHN BAGLOW

McGill-Queen's University Press
Montreal & Kingston • London • Chicago

ISBN 978-0-2280-1848-3 (paper)
ISBN 978-0-2280-1849-0 (ePDF)
ISBN 978-0-2280-1850-6 (ePUB)

Legal deposit third quarter 2023
Bibliothèque nationale du Québec

Printed in Canada on acid-free paper that is 100% ancient forest free
(100% post-consumer recycled), processed chlorine free

Funded by the Government of Canada   Financé par le gouvernement du Canada   Canada   Conseil des arts du Canada   Canada Council for the Arts

We acknowledge the support of the Canada Council for the Arts.

Nous remercions le Conseil des arts du Canada de son soutien.

Library and Archives Canada Cataloguing in Publication

Title: Murmuration: Marianne's book / John Baglow.

Names: Baglow, John, author.

Series: Hugh MacLennan poetry series.

Description: Series statement: The Hugh MacLennan poetry
series | Poems.

Identifiers: Canadiana (print) 20220488614 | Canadiana (ebook)
20220488649 | ISBN 9780228018483 (softcover) |
ISBN 9780228018506 (EPUB) | ISBN 9780228018490 (PDF)

Classification: LCC PS8553.A34 M87 2023 | DDC C811/.54—dc23

This book was typeset by Marquis Interscript in 9.5/13 Sabon.

FOR MARIANNE ELIZABETH MACKINNON

what's in a bubble?
what's just outside it.

keep breathing,
my love.

CONTENTS

Contents

Contents

Contents

MURMURATION

DRYDOCK

*In civilizations without boats, dreams dry up, espionage takes
the place of adventure, and the police take the place of pirates.*
Michel Foucault

and it was in these bare sands
that you fell,
beloved.

rain was a legend;
dust in the basins,
bones in their skin tents –
we made do,
we two

in such heat
that we were haze,
ablaze in the still air
while the curious
tunneled inside
to the four corners of you,
bearing questions and threats

until the dune-ship furrowed up
to take you aboard,
or so i thought.
i woke, i saw the distant wake
in the mirage.

i knew nothing of boats
until the first breeze
set me adrift.

a cracked hull
keeling over the grains
to the dream of water,
hot wind in the sails.

the taint of autumn blights the summer leaves,
so green we were, so bright the summer leaves.

you said, "we were happy, and the world was
blue and green." a delight, the summer leaves.

falling to the year's keen edge, looking back,
longing for one last sight, the summer leaves.

you, your body awry, digging, digging
the garden soil, to right the summer leaves.

birds are shivering in the taut breezes
blowing away the light, the summer leaves.

john awaits his winter; so do we all
this cooler, longer night. the summer leaves.

a spoken word could mine the heart
of its ores and crystals. you are
alive again. in the reeds a bittern
sways with the wind. a star

makes its way through the evening sky,
a speck of yellow dust. it is then
i try to remember.
where were you when

i came to earth?
i found roots in the night
and happened to grow. it was hardly
your fault that i moved out of sight.

lit by the moon, the tinctured windows
hang above us, dimly mark
our vast containment. words
are a sermon in the drafty dark.

GAMBLER

there's no damage: the lighter of you
missed my cheek, the other
let me have it, both barrels,
and missed point-blank.

twice shy to learn the phrase of you,
i gamed and lost
(nothing heals a nonexistent wound
but a green cloth

and something to lose.)
i tried cheating once,
and other languages,
but no rules to break

meant less of a high noon:
a chance word,
an angry face like sunrise
filling my eyes,

but never to the death.
and that's sweet, you think,
that sweetens the pot?
the weapons are dealt: every hand's a loser.

THAT WINTER

no wonder
the fields
are green

it's snowing
inside

THREE SHADOWS

gold

in his hands was a fire
torn from the very soil,
and he sang to the others
like an angel
under the indigo sky.

he never believed
in destinations. long after
he fabled the journey,
all that remained in memory.
sand and shivered stone.

frankincense

he rode like the prince he was,
keeping the others awake
with his jokes and his chatter,
spending his words like a sailor

and so had nothing to say
when he stepped at last through the door.

myrrh

he'll tell you stories,
faces at your window.

he'll speak of what moves
under the snow, under the earth
where the sun lies buried.

he numbers the stars he knew,
the ones he lost on the way.

SIX YEARS

a storm opened beneath us
a wet map, pressing inward

sodden piles of leaves in the yard

the world was in front of us, edging us upward,
and the space you left walks hand in hand

the blossom unfolds like iron, bringing the sea.
voices caught in the blast announce
slow progress to a dead end, still offshore,

then invasion, evacuation
hot winds and blizzards,
dirty water in the veins of cities,
fluent shadows in the half-light for a thousand miles
fire, sleet, candlelight

and beside you i woke,
atlantis, foundered,
already congealing into myth.

i gathered your possessions from our room overlooking
a wood of crows like flakes of burnt paper
and left

still leaving,
looking for higher ground.

time, solo, i went
into a season with intent –
not this, and this,
caught up in the icy nets
and crewed away, bound
for points just off the map.

bear with me, then, held resident
by friends with grizzled cheeks,
the ones
who talk to me of futures.
i arrived, there was a kind of welcome,
then down to it.

thank you, she wrote,
for the picklock in the cake.
others were less than kind
rehearsing their lines by firelight.
no idea, scrivening here,
what on earth's to answer:

i can't hang on to every blessed thing.
no time for that, not any more;
i leave what has to be left
and hurry on – but out of touch somehow,
not making the connection,
never seen or sworn to.

LEAVE-TAKING

(FOR RLB)

a luna battered the glass and left
a pale green husk for the morning,
a shower of summer sparks. you sailed
your stone boat, racing the shadows
into the earth, eager to be away –
and nothing will hold you in these words.

for i with my privilege of words
will facade whatever is left,
and the memories bear you away:
the sun, good as gold in the morning,
too soon is cocooned in shadows,
emerging silver, then bronze ... it sailed

like a damned kite that day, sailed
to hell and gone (o futile words
that blaze and set!), drew shadows
like scars on the dry land you left
(and rose again the next morning,
a pale bubble, drifting away

on the wind). your craft made way,
etching an opal wake; sailed
beyond reach of the morning,
leaving us shorebound. our words
couldn't measure the gap, and were left
to hang in the air and disperse like shadows.

but what is the voice, the image, that shadows
me like a double, pointing the way
with such knowledge, the message you left
in the bottle, cast off as you sailed?
too well i carry those scribbled words
that refuse to come clear in the morning.

we hauled in the anchor, the morning
gull-grey, sloughing its shadows,
so slipped the night's mooring; words
had died with the stars. we got under way,
the breeze picking up, and sailed
that rough beast to the harbours left.

another morning there seemed a way
to follow the shadows where they sailed:
and these words are all i have left.

quick, it always is. your face before
me now. We couldn't embrace before.

one tick, another, a second more
to nightfall – you won the race before.

you swung in the sun, your comet's core
cool, polished like death, a pace before.

now there's only a scatter of shore,
ravenous ocean of space before.

love of a kind: true, not one that tore
soul from rigging, but the chase before.

john, leaving a few words at the door
you rushed through; there was no place before.

RAREE-SHOW

(FOR RGB)

maybe it was the lack
of sober youth, and the flakes
down, down, so they did.
i asked myself, and again,
where long ago i promised.

this was the address,
and no more. behind glass
the strangers kissed. where we had been
in tassels and bows,
so to speak. it's no joke, really

how the answers become,
how they grow around questions
like flowers and vines,
how they reach for our hearts
with too much purpose.

framed in the snow
we're doing our best for
the watching mimes and puppets.
it's the time of year:
dance in these too-heavy costumes,
dance.

some eat your sleep, gulping the hours.
some smile at you through the fog
but never wave back.

sleek light finds the corners
too late.

a fine city, all show and glister,
ramparts and statuary,

the seamless air
embraces.

some toss a few words
like beggars' coin.
you sing what you remember.

what slipped through that wicked wire to the heart?
what set such a monstrous fire to the heart?

years without quench. your body spread out on
a scalding sea plumbs desire to the heart.

what exquisite shapes we carved in the dark,
what epics whispered entire to the heart!

trails are soon overgrown in the wild spring,
meltwater flowing through mire to the heart.

old maps mark our crumbling destinations
and memory is a liar to the heart.

john always ran towards lightning. bright wisps catch
the edge of his mind, retire to the heart.

SHE WANTED

streaky and squalling,
it was,
claiming all of its days.

in the wan autumn light
a leaf does not choose to fall.

things die in october, are buried in winter.
you knew the rules.

in a corner some gifts yet remain:
a bassinet,
a mobile, with stars and the moon.

MARIANNE

there's a little death in there,
in the grounds at the bottom of the cup
in that half-remembered conversation.
the grand gesture; end, begin again.

is this any way to live the days
each with its unwinding spool
of damp, coloured thread?
a bird's cry in the deep woods.

i saw you again in flight
as i was carried on the wind
unable to fall
through this too-solid air.

CHRISTMAS

Sire, he lives a good league hence.

John Mason Neale

endings ...a bleak floor, the fuel spent.
the tense wires of god unplayed in a season.
there were mysteries in the snow
but everything dissolves out of speech,
leaving me breathless.

the awkward visitors came
i ate in silence, the pine-pitch roaring
i watched them becoming song
but plays end, and carols

too long the woods have remained
part of the darkness, unyielding as stone:
i scratch a thin light from a dozen twigs,
scarcely enough to pierce glass,
a light too fragile for blinking.

but on such a night, and such a night
a child lay awake among dreams
and warmed by one star he waited
for the tall words to enter

this light so bright turns everything to glass,
hammers my atoms to pulp in its blind course
to the centre of lead or concrete, makes the gas
glow in its tube, and life a little shorter.
the ancients chose their parallels with care,
it seems – truth was enlightenment that most
avoided, wary of its consummate flame,
and love transformed its object to a ghost.

forgive me then my lesser vision, flawed desire –
windowless towers, quarried to house the world,
adamant walls that give at the slightest question.
names and their shadows pall in the fatal glare;
and some of us take shelter where we learn
to bear a rainbow's brilliant imperfection.

too many friends,
autumn leaves,
blazing, dead.

snowflakes
are burning holes
in the ghosts

and burying
the circus colours.
my words

are freezing
in flight,
unable

to make
the journey
south

where the sun
lies moored.
it's not just you,

perennial
in my thoughts,
or the so many

others,
tethered
to their hills,

but a poinsettia
in the window
braving the season,

blood-red leaves
on the sill,
one by one.

SCARAB

the poem's shell
rang like a bell
bronzish it was
a scarab, with claws

what made the myth
crawl like a bug?
exoskeletal,
a smile on its mug?

and why can i not
stare through its eyes
where my vision is locked,
so robbed of my prize?

mottled with green,
an ancient sheen
colours its task
(no, don't ask)

and so out of sight,
the chitinous rind
leaves with the light,
and so out of mind

R.W.

you slipped behind the moon and hide there still:
breathing night and dust, you abide there still.

half-remembered conversations are all
my words. shell of the past, inside there still.

you lived at no great distance, after all.
Imagine my surprise. (you died there still.)

my rhymes, like rain, like snow: warm, cold they fell
into the hungry earth, a tide there still.

we're all at sea, drifting in our little
painted boats – a wake where you plied there, still.

rita, it's john here, wondering if i
crossed your mind. or am i denied there still?

the spice of new snow pleases the dead.
boulders, ditched by torrents of ice,
are feeding the earth.

this longest dark
i'll add my voice to yours again,
and yours to mine.

the sun slides over the roofs
      weary of light   teeters and falls

now the stars (how i despise
      their knowing looks) peer down at me

a dark room fills with your echo.
      remember when we dared to dream?

blood curls through their runnels,
continents drift

a tortured sky
shakes off its stars

peeling away the layers of light,
one by one by one

it was never easy as pie, this unblinking,
you know, taking it all in at a glance.
the scratch of mineral against mineral,
a little seawater, brought it all together,
what you might call a wet spark
if you insisted,

but the truth is, it was much slower,
more the wearing of rock or the building of rock
until a space opened, an eye,
two. man, it was hard to pry
the lids apart and keep them so,
so very long

and then to look into yours
as if it weren't already a failed task,
this roving eye wanting a horizon:
finding one at last and being one too –
as you told me, the jig was up,
and sleep will not come quickly.

FAUNA

the snail of death is closing the gap,
hot on the scent of our long shadows

the elephant of love leaves ivory
at wrist and throat, and goes where it wills

the mice of war nibble the struts
of wind and wood, the silken tether of lions

smiling, naked, a child sleeps at noon,
fast in the sun's amber

GREEN SHADOWS

(FOR MARIANNE)

in the heat of a spring
we celebrate even
after ten years

old habits refuse to die.
no matter where
the shadows fall

these days,
where dead ends
the map swore

were open spaces
are suddenly met,
think of it all

as a maze,
green
winding hedges,

the sun
at the centre.
i can still

hear your voice.
call to me
again.

ICE AGE

(IN MEMORIAM CAPTAIN L.E.G. OATES)

white where the colours have run.
no trace of me left on the surface;
this ice would never break,
not for the sun and its veins
that could turn the sky to chalk.

ask for no proof of my death:
all trails lead to the body.
i went outside when the world
had no more candles to spare,
and the stars and snow fell together.

LIGHTFALL

sky and cloud promise
rain   bodies dreaming of sweat
embrace the morning

OCTOBER/MARIANNE

remains of green joy:
red and yellow leaves, floating
on the dark water

DECEIT

stars, perfect snowflakes
on the gravemound catching hard
light. the grass erased.

THE MISSING

For three days, she lay dead, partially buried, in a snowbank
at a busy downtown intersection. For three days, a steady stream
of people walked past her. No one noticed the body. Over time,
the falling snow covered her.

News report

dropping quietly out of the conversation.
the thread of it had escaped her,
a subject barely remembered –

we carried on laughing
into the beautiful light
that was falling around us, drifting

ENCOUNTER

in things, memories.

a hard walk to the door,
blinding light
inflaming the brick. (the ragged going their merry way.)
but a good morning, green
for the thousandth time;
pigeons and sparrows
fed out of love
and the fever pitch of the day's events
already on everyone's lips.
                              your name,
mine, parentheses, or carved initials, the tree in silence
growing.

RIDDLES

i.

with a borrowed skin he rides about
in another's pouch, leaving it all too often.
once in a while he roars as he did
but these days he's hungry
and losing his power.
nevertheless, your nimble fingers
rummage his folds for treasure

ii.

a clever beast, helpful at first,
till her family arrives
out of thin air. a peaceful house
will reek of their clamour:
your lover will shun you.
weapons are useless – only your words
can put them to death.

iii.

old chatterbox, living
on ancient wood, won't you take me
where i want to go? do i not feed you,
brush your sleek coat till it shines?
ungrateful, slow-moving wretch,
you swallow me up and pretend to die!

build a lifeform of bricks and mortar,
live for the project you'll become.
it will utter, so the blueprints promise
– well worth waiting for.

have a go at death, but be gingerly,
finding your way back
can be a problem, especially
if you leave the lights off.

try scattering yourself like shot or seed,
wide areas can help you forget.
(weather, too, can snatch you up,
but tends to let go without warning.)

and she has her part to play:
ask her to change the shape
of her absence. it moves, it breathes,
it loves.

  i found i could worship the golden lie … something
comforting about the routine. you called me to account: now
careless with that colour, hard and tasteless as noble metal,
   i sing instead the gunmetal stars in their burning silk
     and our binary path, this work the impossible planet.

   a master falconer set the mind faring forth where it would
to rescue the figures and gists a fabulist, weary of tales too often
enacted, found others with delicate instruments a voice
   in the choir wondered aloud, and would thus resist,
     that the world throw off its liturgy at last;

   and escaper, each prison more spacious, more empty, so few
could follow; boon-companion, the best at argument and chess,
                                                    now silent
as deep space. but everything seems to speak with your voice:
                                              and as words
   themselves lack flesh and so would know you, i would answer
     the clamour, that we both might rest.

we forget even this land is fenced,
so busy as friends; the summer gathered,
a place without news.

slow shift of land against water.
(the conversations resume.)   the buildings
settle into the earth. the sun
burns free of its blue-white gauze
and goes to ground. our various cities
mourn us.
      we forget
what we do, as once
on a hillside, the country gone grey,
we lost a kite in the clouds.

MEMORY

i.

i threw my white bones in the air:
they joined
where I write.

ii.

there were opal waters,
floors the colour
of old honey, a portrait

of welcoming fire ...
a gargoyle sang in its cage
like a cricket:

something of wood
gone green and sinewy
danced on four legs.

iii.

this nest in the attic.
the heart, its
good beginning.

october crashes, saltsea on gravel,
a single voice, body cants, nerve strings played,
a dull decade's rain with sunny intervals.

a. is in another room, tortured with a year-long deathwatch,
works until she dissolves. r. was a false minister.
s. was too little and too late, a fog of commas.

it goes on.

birds volley south. leaves in their tinctured
silence, salting the earth. you were, in your way,
perfect. neither of us knew that.

a weather's guises. your stone in the heart
pointing north.

so we blunder on, abandoned
to the elements, or by them

building-blocks of chaos, so neat
and nice in their proportions

scrawny days and nights, perfervid
weathers, the wretched waters

holding us atop. creatures
in cages, transfixed, silent,

staring at screens. one dove
awaits another, pining.

footfall in the honeycombed hill,
then silence with you at the centre,
hands looking for air, the sky locked out ...
speak to me, my skin burns
with the shreds of light. and i
love you, the sound of the grass growing ...

if i could tell you i would.
the rain has wet me through, the tunnel
opened before me like the sea parting.
i love you, i love you, waiting,
the roots in my hair. lean
into this earth so we can sing again.

SUICIDE

i knew the hollows of things
ran with my blood.

i wanted the light of day,
pure honesty i

put my lips to
the edge of water.

the sweet metal
drips.

my love, my love,
i enter your veins.

mile beyond mile i too bore gifts and found the town shut tight.
but i knew all the signs by heart
and season by season i reached year's end

the door of the hut would not yield; a child's cry within.
my burden grew light as air, but the sun sputtered and caught

there are songs at first sight of green
though the world will ripen and fall;
a harvest returns again to the granary and the manse

once i dreamed i had seen you and looked up to rejoice:
but the skies were filling with unfamiliar stars

RESURRECTION

words cannot speak:

stars
on their taut threads.
i rise, nerveless as gold.

friend, i give incessant love,
a whispering mask.

the riverbank
never came true for me,
the city too close by –
and yet i could dream,
even when we fenced the place,
of rabbits and wolves,
of underground houses
with too many rooms.

so count the leaves and whisper,
friend,
before the first snow
makes our speech too difficult
and the second
takes our breath away.
autumn secrets,
keep them for dear life.

but if years have a way
of ending, for all that,
and stories tell themselves
when we're at a loss for words,
don't believe what you hear.
there's nothing new
under the frost.
speak. take root, like the days.

i have no energy for this
the mercury runs its course down the glass
the coming season is memories,
never timely, drifting where they will

and where we touch the world
it clings we pull away at our peril.
we are too fragile now,
too rooted in the bare rock

but i would like to say to you:

my skin is a seal
against the wind and the falling stars
my flesh is a seabed of dreams
flowering in the darkness·

and my ravenous eyes
will eat light
till the day ends

the motor-laden world
pivots on its coign:
my love and lady, is there
anyone will join
honest hands to grip
the blanket for us all
should we faint and fall?

i hold you like a river,
having, having not.
what we were a season
can obliterate:
the year abandons us,
sowing dragon's teeth
in the soil beneath.

and you will have your words:
the greenest anthems, played
where the snow lies gathered
though elegant echoes fade
with the dwindling sun
to silence for the dawn –
a new year's canon.

and still the winds run wild,
their songs as blue as ice.
so long it is we've looked
each other in the face
to find the lies therein,
all that was done and said:
and seen ourselves instead.

half out of breath.
companion, keep at it,
these moods will drop like a veil.

when summer went bronze
she had my words:
the world disappeared
behind blue shutters

until this air,
silver hooks in the throat.
somewhere a wolf fades to white.

TRANSLATIONS

TRANSLATION

patrick spens

given his orders,
went down to the sea for good

the king who would not
set foot on his own ship
sent him sailing
out of the cottage harbour,

out of the roses

"i am of ireland"

i am of ireland
the holy lands
of ireland

familiar, unfamiliar
streets side by side,
one-legged dancers

come dance with me in ireland

daemon lover

one glance from him
could drown her
where the flowers grow

she shouldn't have come aboard

tall as a mast
he could tear the tender sails,
or break the hull in two

twa corbies

black spots as presented
corvine complement to hot sun

or what is seen by
two dead eyes

hence everywhere and chattering

unquiet grave

do not tempt the mourners to remain

the prayers are over, the shovels
have ceased to clank

while we are gathered,
one word:
you have not died
until that word is ours

so that we too need speak no longer
so that we too may sleep

robin hood

finds his way
into hearts and dossiers

under the bright green canopy
plans his popular strategies
over a stolen meal

keep your eyes wide
those summer afternoons:

begin to notice
the disappearance of loved ones,
the populous forest

edward, edward

the mother knows the father's blood,
her son would not slaughter
his prized animals

giving up the family ruins,
the lands to the weather,
he is already nameless

the sea will wipe his sword clean
there will be other castles

jolly good ale

the songs are cold
as the moon

a man and a woman are smiling

not even silence
can wake them,

nor the gentle night

lord randall

home at last having eaten
the poison – once out of the walls,
he was warned, but went anyway –

he heads for his room,
his mother following
who kept it just as it was

he will sleep in it
forever   she
will die singing lullabies

true thomas

left without a word:
a house stood empty
seven years

thumbing between heaven and hell
where the songs were

we know them by heart

NIGHT JOURNEY

FLOWERS

love is old, love is new

Paul McCartney/John Lennon

i remember the iris, so delicate
a breeze could tear it,
out of harm's way;
and the fire, safe in its niche,
failed to go out.

you had brought everything
into that place, that house,
even the sun disguised as a lamp,
it too with its label –
"on a timer, do not touch."

some of the words were foreign,
some were unspoken, so much
was said over and over like a mantra,
and there were peonies, and strawberries,
and floorboards warped like a ship's hull.

small wonder the new sky
was sketchy with haze,
the world was indoors,
even the lake was an ocean;
there were yellowed maps and we paid no attention,

rumours, fabulous courses,
false history and legend, and still
we could hear the waves touching
a shore that no one had dreamt of,
and a steady wind.

hours, years we sailed
with a bouquet of flowers,
with room after room.
you asked what the voyage meant:
the stars could run us aground,

we know there are ways to lie.
the gods are rocks and thirst,
and nothing with roots would survive
a crossing from land to land.
we begin to taste of salt; all the horizons ebb.

NIGHT JOURNEY

i.

where lamps doubtless
glow like pearls
in ebony. so much
unfamiliar night came down.
given time,

given wine, i rebuilt
that city. watching
two figures
dance in their carved forest,
only our eyes moving.

ii.

in the precious dark
the clock reveals
unheard-of hours.

nothing personal.
red numbers
wasting the shadows.

alive to
this low roof,
abandoned sky

where two of us
went,
seeking shelter.

iii.

it's easier to lie, they lie.
the truth is so simple
it hurts. maybe
not the whole truth

in its acres
of marble columns.
this clean calm where
i practise a second language.

iv.

some nights are like a south wind,
easing the doors wide.

air gone opaque, gentle hands
give welcome.

so learned to believe
the gist of those songs,

you find, you find, you'll
find love where the rainbows end.

go blindfold. show me
where your heart is poised.

v.

not thinking ahead.
i tasted death before. haven't yet
snagged this idiom,
things trying to grow
just out of sight. don't
look now.

no end of words to praise you,
to settle the matter,
deep in black crystal
like comets.
touching wherever you are, this
tentative light.

winter

i would not be foolish
to build your image of snow.
the sun will have us both by and by.
accept, then, this bloodless copy, my love turned ritual;
nerves in ice, it takes this to speak.

spring

naked, we fled
the white shelter;
the sun at its best
would craze the blank mirror,
spilling the year into its channel:
and this was before
the words became restless in their great, hot rooms.

in anger, in love
the ground breaks:
confessions
in the smoky light.
a wood yields, leaf by leaf,
slow turns of the grain.
under wet acres
the moon stirs like a seed.

summer

the sun would skip a beat,
merrily the planet stagger
and right, the zodiac hum like a prayer wheel;
or the earth turn slowly on its spit,
near done. whatever.

these nights like dominoes in a box,
time between then and then.
hundreds of green miles
grow and flourish.
the stranded cities come out like stars.

fall

for the soil, the sand
this handful of flames
fair exchange,

nourishing heat.
my songs flee south,
glyphs against zinc,

the whole sky
wanting
your eyes.

POSSESSION

i.

in the twilight two
figures dance:
one is of wood

the other – well,
could be you
or i, holding on

for dear love,
the fierce grain
leaving its mark

(we pretend
to ignore
the signs

there have been
such gods
at work)

all of us
will embrace
the mute

spirits
for whatever
reason

and i,
caught thus,
do not start

at the sound
of your
voice

ii.

graven images:
what is done,
what is past

what is not.
step carefully
among ruined

jaws and fingers
you thought
were statuary

cool moves.
do not
adore these words.

iii.

this creature
faces existential dilemmas
not of his making,

and wreaks bad movies
on the innocent.
believe me when i
tell you:

somewhere
blood flows
in the proper channels.

iv.

how well i know
the articles of faith
and all the wicked weapons –

the means
to drive me out,
to leave mere substance

untormented. come,
dance with me
for the time it takes.

RETURN TRIP

as i suspected, the highways really led nowhere.
the house lay aground amid its black ribbons,
another point of departure;
and loving too fast would end in disorder, then
dreams of miles before daybreak.

we excel in geography:
i, with my love of the map's edge,
you with your marksman's eye;
and our thirty-odd years of momentum
that could make each encounter the last one.

you treasure the journals i keep: the traces of you and me,
like fossils in porcelain – there were days
the whole countryside sparkled.
we wake in that cold light.
i aim for your heart like an arrow.

HIROSHIMA MON AMOUR

where our skins touched
we fused like melting glass

the light was too perfect
we etched the surroundings with shadows

we stared at each other seeing only
the far unblemished horizon before

the two of us spilled like wax among
the ghosts of rocks and flowers

GOODBYE

of course nothing ends this way: there's only one
final line (which rhymes
with everything)

nothing comes to an end like this, so perfectly you can feel
the hand of an artist
draw that world to a close –

how easily you unstitched
the embroidered curtain
where earth and sky were joined. as if i needed the air.

12 PARABLES

The rock

Once a rock, observing the world whirl by, desired to be
alive like the wind, like leaves caught up in the gusts, like
snowflakes. He was less interested in plants, somewhat
more in animals, but wanted to be freer than both.

All rocks are male. They can change, but not reproduce.
They are hard, and incessant. What doesn't kill them
turns them to sand, and ultimately earth.

Beside him, a tree began to sprout. The twig rubbed
against the rock, and gave it magic powers. He could feel
veins, hunger, and a deep throbbing.

Reflected in a nearby pool were two trees, entwined.
Their branches had grown together. In the breeze they
made a sound like sobbing, but they seemed aglow.

The rock could feel the tree growing next to him.
Somehow she (for the tree was a she) was causing him to
live. He wanted to embrace her, but had no limbs. Inside,
at his core, he grew molten. He thought he would spill
out through his weathered skin, through the crude lichens
that had scarred him over the years, and the moss on his
northern side.

The rock half-sensed the reflection of the two ecstatic
trees. And he became aware that the tree, pressed against
him, was aware of it as well.

He could feel the tree's roots spread slowly under him. He felt on fire, as he had felt the heat from countless forest fires in his time. He began to split apart, but it was a joyous feeling, and he welcomed it.

He thought he flowed around the tree at his side, remembering his hot formlessness before he was shaped. But she was growing into him, reshaping him, splitting what must be split. He gave, and groaned in the giving. He was hers now.

Her leaves spread above him in a glorious canopy. He slept.

The clock

Every hour and five minutes, the big brass hand of the old ebony clock closes over the small hand, for one delicious interval. But the two are always joined, even as they separate: they are together at the centre of the clock where time begins and ends.

Kept brightly polished, the two lived longer than the maker. So many years ago they were taken from the dust of an old antiquarian shop, soon demolished to make way for a fancy bicycle store. Placed in the bedroom of a lovely new house, they measured time for the couple that occupied the bed.

It all seemed innocent enough. The ways of humans were not the ways of a clock and its hands.

One night the hands heard the man ask his much younger partner, "Why are you looking at the clock?" The hands, in their ecstatic 11:55 embrace, suddenly felt something they had never felt before – shame.

After that, their momentary conjunctions grew hateful to them. And yet they remained joined, forever, as the clock whirred and ticked. They began to feel as if they were under a curse.

One day the clock began making new, jarring sounds. Soon the hands felt heavy, and time slowed. A final metallic creak and they stopped, precisely at midnight.

"Why fix that thing?" asked the man to his perky young partner. "It looks lovely as it is, and I can do without the ticking and tocking – and you looking at it all the time."

It is not recorded whether the couple, or the hands in their permanent embrace, grew to live happily ever after.

The mirrors

The two mirrors had just been hung in a small and fairly dark room: their reflected light helped lessen the gloom a little. They were on opposite walls, and opposite corners, so they could only imagine what their own reflections might look like.

They knew that they each reflected light, and the images of the man and woman who stood before them, sometimes in admiration, sometimes critically. Their best understanding was that they were somehow able to give back what came to them: other than that, they had no real idea what a reflection was.

Mirrors have their own life, and the ability to love. After all, they see the world and present it as it is, if reversed. So it was not long before the two mirrors began a silent conversation, mostly consisting of questions at first.

The mirror with the large oak frame asked: Who are you? And the smaller mirror in the faux-ivory frame, a badly-judged wedding present, asked: Who wants to know?

It's hard to say who you are when you don't know who you are. Mirrors are everything but themselves, or so it seems to them. But the two soon learned what needs to be learned. Each told the other what they could see – what they were reflecting. Their silence was a glow of meaning. They were in love, without knowing what that was or how to express it.

Finally they told each other of their dreams, for mirrors can dream. Each wanted to see the other, to be reflected in the other, to merge in a burst of silvery light.

One day the couple ventured into their small bedroom and were displeased with what they saw. Dingy wallpaper and still a trifle dark, it was not a welcoming bower of bliss. "If both mirrors were only closer to the window," said the woman. "Let's move Martha's present to the left."

The mirrors hardly dared hope. Soon the little one
had been repositioned, the man – a burly sort – standing
between it and the oak-framed one. He stood aside,
pleased.

The two mirrors did not merge. They saw infinite
reflections of each other. Which were real? But no
reflections are real. They saw themselves, the other in
themselves, themselves in the other in themselves ...

Joy? Madness? They had no way of telling.

Soon enough it was nightfall, and then the lamp in the
room was turned off. They could barely wait for the
next sun to rise.

The book

In a story you never head in a straight line from page
one to the last word. You find yourself remembering bits
and pieces of it and new twists emerge: there are
reverberations and echoes as you go. The thread moves
backwards and forwards in time as you turn leaf after
leaf in sequence.

But what of the pages themselves?

Once, in a very old romantic story, there were two,
separated by many others, who managed to conjoin,
throwing the book into an uproar.

The first introduced the heroine, Maria Marguerite. The second covered, in short and frantic syllables, an account of the hero's battle with a gang of bandits. His name was Juan Calderón. He won, but that's not important – it's what heroes do, and he had no choice in the matter.

Nor is the story all that important either. It was one of those tales where all is fixed, the ending is inevitable, the characters fall into line as the author orders.

But the pages have a life of their own that is less well

understood. They tell their own tale, a tangled one, with no beginning or end.

Some say that all the pages ever written and printed, and those still to come, are one glorious story that explains the universe and everything in it: but only the pages themselves can read it.

The Maria page and the Juan page somehow fell in love, if by that we mean they desired to entangle the narratives that they bore. And soon you could barely follow the twistings and turnings – how Maria fought with a bandit who turned out to be her hero, Juan; how the others conspired to attack them both at a crossroads; how she was very beautiful, and was looking for a nameless hero; how two brigands fell in love with each other after catching sight of a woman neither of them could love.

The other pages were not pleased with this turn of events. On them, the story writhed and twisted uncomfortably. They were used to interpretations: when the storyline faded, when one path became brightly lit and another dimmed, when characters had ambiguous motives, or perhaps none at all, for their actions.

But to have the characters switch places, take on each other's identities, fall in love in a paragraph when otherwise the tale was silent – all that and more caused the rest of the story enough concern to get the pages itching.

What was to be done? The tale demanded that the pages be kept separate – but they already were. What was joining them together in this riotous skein of bliss? The mind of a crazy-bright reader who happened to be inching down the story's trail, carving a few of his own on the way? Some magical property of the glue in the spine, opening up channels where none should be?

No one will ever know, of course. A brief emergency meeting was held. Then the pages struck a massive blow, briefly allowing all the words on their surfaces to merge in a pool of ink. The tincture soaked all of the pages, including the two infatuated ones who had no idea what was coming until it was too late.

Their entwined narratives were engulfed. Not a word was legible. The stain confused them. They forgot who or what they were. They lost their numbers. It was as though creation was moving backwards, into the primordial dark from which all things once emerged.

Then, in an instant, the words reappeared: through a prodigious act of recall, the pages channeled the ink back into the shallow grooves left by the letters before all the trouble started. The words formerly borne by the two troublesome ones were once again securely in place.

Having lost their memories of themselves and each other, they no longer cared to disrupt the old tale with the new and sometimes wonderful revisions that had marked their love. They carried their part of the story on their backs, and did so silently and patiently, until the yellowed leaves crumbled into dust.

The scissors

The two blades, joined at the hip, live only to close, becoming one – and let nothing come between them!

Paper – the possessor of records, lies, reports and captured dreams – has learned this to its cost. What may carry the dread power of an entire system stamped upon it will yield to the scissors.

Larger ones trim hedges; smaller ones, moustaches. Ecstatic pairs of blades may be found where other implements dare not wander.

Stone is their enemy. In truth they avoid each other, having nothing in common.

But scissors, cutting paper, are multi-orgasmic.

The waves

Waves travel, but what they pass through remains more or less in place.

But that's mere physics. Waves endlessly chase each other, into space and onto beaches. We are deeply stirred, but always fail to grasp the object of our affections. He or she is ever out of reach, always just ahead or just behind.

Until we crash upon the shore in a brilliant tangle of light and spray.

The ring

A ring is both open and closed: it can wear the whole universe until it is placed upon a single finger.

No tail, no mouth, no snake: seamless, endless, one infinity among many. Or a shackle, a single binding link in a chain that grows ever-longer.

I circle you, dancing. You embrace me.

The masks

Wood, feathers, metal, clay, learning to speak. Bone, flesh, rushing blood, learning to speak.

Masks wearing masks.

What peers out from them, doing the endless ceremonial steps?

Once before time, there was only the ritual. It pined for substance so that it could be real, without knowing what it meant to be real.

When everything came to be, it was scattered in pieces across the sky. When the world was formed, and life swam out of the sea to be closer to the sun, it remained separated from itself.

The two lovers gaze at each other across a chasm, masks reflecting the stars. And when they touch, the healing of the ritual begins.

The river

We are on a raft, carried by an unknown river. We pass through white water into quieter miles of green, and then into wider reaches more like a lake, barely moving.

Sometimes I wake to find myself on dry land, you drifting by on the raft we shared. I fear a sudden bend will take you out of sight. Or, I am alone on the water: I see you walking deep in the fields beyond the banks before you disappear into some trees in the further distance.

These may be dreams.

It's an adventure, you say. Let's go wherever it takes us.

Two cliffs, stone walls. Then trackless open spaces, miles inland a small town or perhaps a jumble of stones glinting pale in the early afternoon sunlight. Water lilies, riversmell, a fish jumping at a dragonfly. A snapping turtle snoozing on a muddy promontory, a nearby chorus of frogs safe in a patch of reeds.

We look at each other but we see only the river in each other's eyes.

The winds

The north wind, cold, sleek, dry, encounters the moisture-laden tropical south wind, and the two soak the earth with cool rain.

Far below, people open umbrellas. Roofs sparkle with crazed light from the street lamps.

The fish

From an all-round window that he can't see, a fish observes the refracted world.

Is there another like him? How did he come to be?

He feels desire without knowing what he desires, or even that he is feeling it. It's part of his natural state, like his confinement, the bright overhead lights, the vague sounds on the other side of the glass, filtered through water.

He does not feel confined.

The Task

The two lovers encountered the Task around a loop in the road that they had been travelling together, hand in hand.

They stopped. A stone has blocked our way, she said.

That's not a stone, it's a sleeping Task, he said. Let's try not to wake it.

But it was too late. Feed me, said the Task.

What do you eat? asked the woman.

Love, said the Task.

Then there is more than enough for you right here, she said.

No, said the Task. You are keeping it to yourselves.

They embraced the Task. They became graffiti, like the ones you see unfinished on roadside rockfaces. A scrawl where lovers paused.

THROUGH A RED LENS

his favourite colour is mauve

he's got a horse in a distant valley
and a *pied-à-terre* in london

he wakes at the first squawk of light
calling his beasts by name: thunder! lightning! –
until he remembers, and sleeps

and others remember too:
out of tune with the times, he is,
a streak of ruby in the polar sky
set to the common music,
a patient man, snowed under,
labouring at his bench
in wood and plastic and gold

i saw him hunched in the crowds
at the corner of two windy streets
needing a bit of change, so he said,
it's the season of rough weather, it's rough all over,
and his voice was a thin sing-song

why not? he sang, why not?
i loved you once
in the days i could call
my crazy name to my mind;
but all that's left of me now
i gave i gave i gave

NAILED TO THE MOON

i look down
at the pocked streets
of gaza,

craters
no matter the size
open

like skin,
bleeding dust into
dust

"KENNEBUNKPORT, MAINE"

(FOR JOEL KROPF)

boutiques bursting with river-fog,
the tourist canopies blurred,
too-heavy souvenirs
falling from the hand.

at the fable's marge
the sidewalks resume
their concrete manoeuvres.
weeds, errant flies,

you and i.
but a president walked
naked under the
stainless spires,

the fortress aching with summer heat,
marble-white pavement
searing the eyes
under birdless, cloudless skies.

a taste of bread and chowder
on the terraces,
crisp linen brought to the lips
to hold the words in.

heaven was like this
way back when:
speechless, rarified.
out of ken.

MILLENNIUM

footsteps echo in an empty room
a room as big as a country.
glaciers pointed the way once.
count the zeroes in the year 2000.

south is where the work went
lightspeed down a wire.
further south the bosses burn.
(ozone starts with a zero.)

fly me, try me, buy me
for a meal or a pair of shoes.
i can speak anything going –
all borders dissolve in tears.

who is living on the green estates?
who gives us our daily bread?
who has mastered the art
of squeezing our blood from stones?

There's more than meets the eye.
we left ourselves at the border.
we left our names where they fell.
nothing could stop us.

SPECIALIST

Several street beggars were picked up whose disappearance
would attract no attention. This was a technique that (Daniel)
Mitrione had developed or rather perfected in Brazil. Using these
beggars, experiments were conducted with the different forms
of interrogation, letting the students see the effect of different
voltages on different parts of the body, male and female.
All these unhappy people died without really knowing why
they were undergoing this pain. Without even having the
cowardly solution of answering any questions because they
were not asked any.

Manuel Hevia

to nurture the human voice, observing strict standards,
as some would uncoil, unkink
the myriad strands
of space, of dreams.

so do we labour for wisdom,
if often we gain
mere knowledge. i too reject
all partisan burdens,
if not the too-human joy

when sheer sound resolves into syllables, grammar,
good sense – the pride of a father, hearing at last
his infant's first word.

and so did our ancestors struggle out of their hairy skins,
all nerves awake
where the sky's bright fingers played their delicate discords:

faces marbled with rain and light, they uttered:
the universe poised
far above them, old as the rocks, hungry for invocation.

MUSIC IN THE STREETS

(1991 PSAC GENERAL STRIKE)

gilded cadenzas, hammered
arpeggios, the brilliant piano
a flash of colour in a crafted sea
of brass and wind –

> we'll have all that
> too. even now, we shape
> how we lived the time, what
> to remember, to tell,
> we steer those days
> into myth. no matter:

we did write the music ourselves,
the music we found in the streets,
the *vox humana*, a rising wave,
a chorus to crack the smug silence –

> and working the past to our liking,
> retracing our millions of steps,
> the composer's mind is still playing:
> a phrase or two, an inkling of rhythm,
> the thing gets better and better:
> it's classic before you know it.

i.

a lake you wanted, a peaceful one,
your mast like a needle
at the centre but a careless coin
would send a tidal wave,
or so the tricks of memory.

                           it was all
a dance my feet remember,
virtuoso words in corners now and then,
salt at the rim, the cold night sky
with one eye open. moon-wax, why not
a pale amber to slither about on,
and lost it entirely

                     and so to a dream
set somewhere in a mile-high empty house,
the winds beginning and ending inside
the monstrous walls. you wanted a lake, you said,
but knowing me ...

ii.

to another anniversary,
a tidy affair if you keep your wits,
a day you can't lie your way out of
no matter how warm it gets

                     hearts beat as one,

or so insists
the humming wire, the excellent mimic
we learned to love. atop a tree an angel
watches our every move. smell the resin.
in all this inside weather, the scattering of pieces,
a cold spell can be banished
with ancient wisdom.

through a red lens i could see
a beggar station himself
at the stable door, waiting
for the year to end, rubbing
his one good eye.

the world on our weary shoulders
rubbed raw by the days of our lives:
shall we set the burden down at last?
shall we head to town for one big blast?
shall we drink the spirits till we drop?

how will the earth spin? how will the sun rise?

who cares? they belong to somebody else,
let them pull the string, make the chimes ring,
anchor the pulleys that make it all run,
light the candles of star and sun
and drag the moon through its wax and wane.

what of the holy chant, the beads and incense?

hide in your cells as we live in ours,
scraping the ground for roots, drinking the bitter rain.
we'll wrestle your angels to earth again
and sing new cities into being
with our beads of sweat, our incense of raw onions.

TWO THOUSAND

what could live in a hollow moon?
light, yellow with age? dust?
it hangs in the sky by a thread,
everyone knows.
the rest is mere history.

fragile, these times. a moment
to hear heartbeats
somewhere in deep space.
not to surrender on these shores.
to say no, and again, no.

a few scruffy birds
peck for scarce grain
in a bitter shiver of wind.
dead leaves whirl in the yard
where a snowman is dreaming of flowers.

FISH OUT OF WATER

(Reading Warsan Shire's "Home")

there is no home
at the other end of this.
another step, and those never end,

or being pulled along
in the current,
or pushed by fear,

blood in the water.
there can be no destination,
only out of here

around the next bend
and the next, and the next –
no wonder you take the leap

out of faith, out of ken,
a shoal on the shore, drowning
in all the freedom of air.

yell when the ear is near, dear,
but the mouth has got no teeth;
the tongue at its moor of sinew
tugs at the jaw beneath.

nor if it is public or private,
an organ can't compete
when the pulse rate drops to this level –
even the feet must eat.

so head for the heart for a start, dear,
(nudge the bad blood aside)
a true thrust is a trust, love,
a wrong is a right denied.

a shot in the dark will never go wide
though our hands be as cold as death:
the brain must come to a standstill
if the mind is to catch its breath.

KIM, KIM, KIM

Il-sung is still
served under glass,
Now Jong-il's dead –
All things must pass

The people weep,
As they do each day
Future and past
One shade of grey:

Anything new
Under the son
Now Kim the Third
Is Numero Un?

horizon, shrouding a glow in the dark.
night within night, what will grow in the dark?

the moon's expenditure. so weary, now,
feasting on flesh. cold winds blow in the dark.

reports echo. blind, groping, soon enough
we learn what skeletons sow in the dark.

all of us are waging war in our way,
reaping a harvest of snow in the dark.

it's getting late. windows are mirrors now.
we are consoled: blood will flow in the dark.

john can barely see your face, so long past
his love. knowing what we know in the dark.

ORANGE ALERT

i.

where do the winds come from?
dogs, entitled to nothing, howl at the moon.
days, pale and wet, give way to night.

wending the corridors and streets,
the lights a harsh blur;
i can hardly make you out.

water's a memory under the ice.
are you there too in the green gloom
remembering?

ii.

great battles were fought
the great wars were won:
we're all refugees,
look away, look away.

don't give it a thought
we're done, we're all done.
stay silent, be safe.
look away, look away.

we've tasted the food
the water, the wine –
everything's fine.
look away, look away.

'tis the season, rejoice.
good friends, charge your glass:
here's to you, and to you.
look away, look away.

iii.

we must have crossed paths,
the errands we run:
a wisp of smoke, a falling star,
a nod or a whisper,
bells in the crisp morning air.

no trick, this speech without words:
it's a matter of celebration,
we're all getting down to it.
never mind what we can afford,
there's a song at stake, and we're singing.

barbarians in greasy clothing, spending the night here,
before they move on, hoarse and restless, ending the night here.

a flag-tainted progress of fools, roasting pigs in the streets,
they partied till morning, harsh music rending the night here.

order, of a kind, was restored. we can feel their absence:
empty air, a sky full of stars mending the night here.

something is left unfinished in their going. just a pause
in the old war: the lines are drawn, transcending the night here.

well-wishers are nursing their grudges, now *in pectore*,
so bitter their moon, february tending the night here.

with friends, john awaits a reckoning. surely it's coming.
shadows prowl in the dark: we're all befriending the night here.

UNFINISHED

BREAK

you will not heal
in your metal works,
a tin box
fashioned so

and the things
you brought
weigh
like too many beads

these years,
lapsing
and relapsing,
a possession

a demon
at rusty controls
steering
over broken stones

cursing,
afflicted,
beset.
i love you.

BACKGAMMON

snow wraps
the world tight this evening,

too tight to breathe
after weeks

of watching him drift
like a ghost ship

losing way in the time and weather,
st. elmo's fire in his head.

just out of reach
like a memory,

his hand trembles
from cut nerves

and his mask is a face
that speaks air.

he throws the dice,
and we begin.

DANNY

if there is a future,
the gods likely know it:
what else is there to think about,
or do?

out of their rheumy eyes
they watched my sweet kid fall to earth,
and said nothing.

what, after all, is there to say?
language is for those
so sure of themselves
they must protest.
but those who know what's coming

are the ones full of doubts:
they can change not a thing
and wonder what they might have done
unchained

because it took four seconds for you
to hit the ground, more or less,
smashing yourself on the concrete facedown
and the greenstone pendant i gave you

and because that time
contains a whole life closed to me,
i am not a poet anymore.
i live in the dark now, casting no shadow.

memories are all my stars
flaming out as they fell,
chunks of half-molten iron and stone
shapeless, broken,

only what they were.
nothing can warm the heart
still beating, beating,
in its wine-dark sea.

under the autumn sky
a tree raises its bare branches
to catch the rain,
and these words hang in midair

MISSING

i don't know where the flowers end up
let alone *les neiges d'antan*,
but there's new snow on the ground
and a dog is bounding over a wet white hill.

the field below lies draped
over knives of rock
and the dog disappears like the day,
finding its home.

night is thick with cold,
windless, quiet as the moon.
the stars in their cages are pacing,
but free them, and they will fall.

ACKNOWLEDGMENTS

Some of these poems have appeared in *Our Times,*
Literary Review of Canada, Wascana Review, Capilano
Review, Antigonish Review, Malahat Review, The Café
Review, and *Eastern Structures.*